D0773766

SECRET OF THE PLANT-KILLING ANTS

. . . AND MORE!

BY ANA MARÍA RODRÍGUEZ

Enslow Publishers, Inc.
40 Industrial Road
Box 398
Berkeley Heights, NJ 07922
USA

http://www.enslow.com

Acknowledgments

The author would like to express her immense gratitude to all the scientists who have contributed to the *Animal Secrets Revealed!* series. Their comments and photos have been invaluable to the creation of these books.

Library of Congress Cataloging-in-Publication Data

Rodriguez, Ana Maria, 1958–
  Secret of the plant-killing ants— and more! / Ana María Rodríguez.
    p. cm. — (Animal secrets revealed!)
  Summary: "Explains why ants in the Amazon rain forest kill all but one species of plant and details other strange abilities of different types of animals"—Provided by publisher.
  Includes bibliographical references and index.
  ISBN-13: 978-0-7660-2953-8
  ISBN-10: 0-7660-2953-0
  1. Ants—Juvenile literature. 2. Ants—Research—Juvenile literature. I. Title.
QL568.F7R63 2009
595.79'6—dc22

                              2007039494

Printed in the United States of America

10 9 8 7 6 5 4 3 2 1

To Our Readers: We have done our best to make sure all Internet Addresses in this book were active and appropriate when we went to press. However, the author and the publisher have no control over and assume no liability for the material available on those Internet sites or on other Web sites they may link to. Any comments or suggestions can be sent by e-mail to comments@enslow.com or to the address on the back cover.

♻ Enslow Publishers, Inc., is committed to printing our books on recycled paper. The paper in every book contains 10% to 30% post-consumer waste (PCW). The cover board on the outside of each book contains 100% PCW. Our goal is to do our part to help young people and the environment too!

Illustration Credits: Dr. Megan Frederickson, Stanford University, pp. 30, 32, 34; Jupiterimages Corporation/Photos.com, pp. 8, 24; Dr. Wah-Keat Lee, Argonne National Laboratory, p. 6; Dennak Murphy, p. 13; Herbert A. "Joe" Pase III, Texas Forest Service, Bugwood.org, p. 15; Dr. Scott Powell, pp. 37, 39, 40, 41; Drs. Tom Richardson and Nigel Franks, University of Bristol, p. 22; Alex Wild, p. 17.

Cover Illustration: Alex Wild.

★ CONTENTS ★

ENTER THE WORLD OF ANIMAL SECRETS!

This volume of *Animal Secrets Revealed!* will show you incredible things ants do. Begin your journey in a physics lab where American scientists use very powerful X-rays to "see" what happens inside tiny insects when they breathe.

Travel with other American scientists to the desert of New Mexico and discover how ants smell one another's jobs using chemical "business cards." Move on to a lab in Bristol, England, where scientists have set up a special arena to study ants going to school. Animals can learn, but can they teach?

Accompany a young American scientist as she uncovers the mystery behind devil's gardens in the Amazon rain forest of Perú. Is it really an evil spirit that creates them?

Finally, travel to Panamá, where British scientists spend hot and humid summers studying how army ants create high-speed trails to bring "fast food" to the colony. Welcome to Animal Secrets!

1
BUGS SQUEEZE TO BREATHE

Wah-Keat Lee was in the physics lab testing a new technique that used X-rays to see the insides of objects. But these were no ordinary X-rays, like those you may find at a doctor's office. Lee was using one of the strongest X-ray machines in existence, the synchrotron.

The synchrotron has a circumference of about 1 kilometer (0.62 miles), the length of about ten football fields. It accelerates electrons almost to the speed of light. When electrons travel that fast, they produce different kinds of radiation, including X-rays. Synchrotron X-rays are more than one billion times as intense as conventional X-rays used by doctors.[1]

Lee thought that the superpowerful X-rays would probably allow him to create images of the insides of objects with much more detail than the images created by regular X-rays. What could he use to test the X-ray vision of this powerful machine?

Lucky Insect

Lee found a dead ant and placed it in the path of the X-ray beam. He started the machine, and the powerful rays passed through the ant's body. An image appeared on the screen. Lee was amazed.

He saw the ant's internal organs with sharp detail. This level of detail had never been achieved before with any other

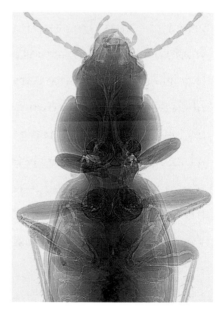

These photos show how the same beetle, called *Pterostichus*, looks on the outside and on the inside. The image at right is an X-ray taken using the synchrotron.

technique. He could see the ant's inside body parts very clearly. He described it in this way: "It's almost as if parts of the anatomy have been outlined in pencil, like a drawing in a coloring book."[2]

The dead ant turned out to be Lee's lucky insect. It helped him discover an important application, or use, for the powerful X-rays. Lee realized that the X-rays would be very useful to entomologists, or insect scientists. The synchrotron would allow them to see inside tiny living creatures with a level of detail that was unknown before. So Lee searched the Internet for a biologist working on insects who might be interested in using the synchrotron. He found Mark Westneat, and other scientists, with whom he has been working ever since.[3]

> **Meet the Scientists:** *Wah-Keat Lee is a physicist (an expert in physics, the field of science that deals with matter and energy and how they interact) who works with advanced machines like the synchrotron. The synchrotron is located at Argonne National Laboratory in Argonne, Illinois. Mark Westneat is a biologist who is interested in learning how the internal body parts of tiny insects and other creatures work. He works at the Field Museum in Chicago, Illinois.*

Insides in Action

One of the things that makes the synchrotron a groundbreaking tool is it can be used on living beings under certain conditions

Beetles and roaches (above) are among the many insects who "squeeze to breathe."

without harming the creatures. Furthermore, the powerful technique allows scientists to see and record still images and also videos of the insides of tiny insects.[4] Scientists are able to see how the internal parts move and work in a living insect without cutting it open. The synchrotron provided a new way to look at how the insides of living creatures work.

Squeeze to Breathe

Westneat, Lee, and their colleagues decided to use synchrotron X-rays to try to see how insects breathe. Scientists knew that insects use a system of tubes called tracheae to deliver air to their organs. The tracheae connect to the outside of the body through holes called spiracles, which insects open and close.

Scientists also knew that air moves in and out of the insect's body by simple diffusion or passive movements when insects are resting. When insects are active and need more air to breathe, they use their air sacs. The insect's body movements make air sacs inside its body pump more air through the tracheae.[5] Scientists knew the tracheae are soft, but do they actually squeeze the air when insects breathe?

The scientists irradiated a live ant with the X-rays and then observed the video recording of the ant breathing. They saw that the flexible tracheae actually compressed and expanded, helping move the air in and out of the body through the spiracles. Nobody had described seeing the tracheae squeezing air before.[6]

Ants squeeze to breathe. They breathe in a way similar to that of creatures with lungs. They rhythmically pump air in and out of their bodies as they contract and expand their air sacs and tracheae.

A New Way to Look Inside Insects

Besides ants, the scientists studied beetles, crickets, butterflies, cockroaches, and dragonflies. All of them squeeze to breathe.[7] The synchrotron has changed the way scientists can look inside insects. The powerful X-rays allow scientists to study the internal organs of tiny living creatures and find out how they work. For example, scientists are studying how insects use their complex internal mouth parts to trap prey and process their food.[8] By using the synchrotron in creative ways, scientists have provided us with the clearest picture yet of how insects breathe.

2
ANTS HAVE BUSINESS CARDS

It is 4:30 A.M. The sun has not risen yet, but Deborah Gordon has. She is wearing her long, thick socks over the cuffs of her pants. She has learned that the socks-over-cuffs strategy prevents most ants from getting up her pants.

Gordon adjusts her light-colored, long-sleeve shirt. She picks up her cap, which has a flap on the back side to shield her neck from the scorching desert sun. She grabs the largest sunglasses she can find. She will wear them later, when the sun comes up. Gordon wrote once that she "looked rather like an insect" herself.[1] She will meet many ants as she surveys about three hundred colonies spread over a desert patch, each one individually marked with painted stones.

Colonies Without a Leader

Gordon has been studying a society of ant colonies in Rodeo, New Mexico, for about twenty years. In this time, she has focused on a particular species, or kind, called the red harvester ant. Up to about twelve thousand red harvester ants live in a single nest.[2] Each ant is about half a centimeter (0.2 inch) long. This is about one-third the diameter of a dime. There is one queen in each nest, and the rest are workers with various jobs.

Some workers live in the deepest parts of the underground nest. They take care of the queen and her eggs.

Other workers enlarge the nest, while maintenance workers keep it clean. They bring all the waste, including dead ants, outside the nest.[3] Workers change tasks. They move from one task to the next as they get older or if more ants are needed for a particular task.[4]

> **Science Tongue Twister:**
> *The red harvester ant's scientific name is* **Pogonomyrmex barbatus.**

Gordon has been particularly interested in two other types of workers called patrollers and foragers. Patrollers scout the foraging area every morning, and the foragers collect food for the colony.

Amazingly, thousands of ants manage to keep their colony working without a boss. The queen, in spite of her title, does not rule. She spends her life in the deepest chambers of the nest laying eggs. She does not surface to supervise or direct the activities of the numerous ants.[5] How do ants know what to do? Foragers and patrollers will reveal their secret.

Foragers and Patrollers

Gordon has been interested in how foragers know when it is time to go out and collect seeds for the colony. If ants could talk, a scientist's work would be easier. Ants do not talk, but they do perform their activities regularly. Scientists can learn a lot about ants' lives by carefully observing their activities.

Dr. Gordon is sitting at the center of the hole digging up an ant colony to bring to the lab, and she just found the queen. Dr. Gordon's daughter (standing behind Dr. Gordon) named the queen "Molly."

Gordon and her colleagues have observed that red harvester ants begin their activities when the sun rises. (That is why Gordon and her colleagues get up so early.)

When the first sunrays begin to warm the dry desert land, maintenance workers emerge from the nest carrying waste in their mouths. They deposit it in a pile outside the nest. Patrollers come out too, and explore the surroundings of the nest. When patrollers come back, foragers leave the nest. They follow trails looking for seeds to bring back home. This routine happens practically every day.

One of the most intriguing things about red harvester ants is that foragers will not leave the nest if patrollers do not return. Only when patrollers come back, and not other workers, like maintenance ants, will foragers leave. It is like the no-return of the patrollers is a message to foragers that it is not safe to go out.[6] So they stay home for the rest of the day. How do they recognize patrollers?

Like Chemical Business Cards

Red harvester ants do not see very well, and sound does not seem to be very important for their communication either. Instead, these ants communicate with chemical and tactile, or touch, messages. They keep in constant communication with other ants by smelling one another with their antennae. Some of the scents tell them whether an ant belongs to their colony or to a different one. The red harvester ant also has chemicals

Harvester ants at work at the nest entrance.

on its surface that are like a person's business card; they indicate what type of job the ant does.

Some of these chemicals are called hydrocarbons.[7] They are similar to wax and coat the ant's cuticle, which is the external layer of its body. A red harvester ant has about twenty-five different cuticular hydrocarbons, which other red harvester ants can smell with their antennae.

Ants with different jobs smell different. The reason is that the proportion of the different hydrocarbons on an ant's surface changes with the ant's job. Maintenance workers have a chemical business card, or smell, that is different from the patrollers' smell. Was it possible that the detection of the patrollers' smell—their chemical business card—was the signal foragers needed to leave the nest?

Smelly Glass Beads

To test this idea, Gordon and her colleague Michael Greene tried to trick foragers into leaving the nest using tiny beads that smelled like patrollers.

Gordon and Greene arrived at the nest at sunrise each morning. First, they collected all the patrollers before they went back into the nest and engaged in antennal contact with foragers. Then, the scientists simulated patrollers coming back into the nest. They dropped 3-millimeter-wide (0.12-inch-wide) glass beads coated with patrollers' scent into the nest entrance, where foragers were waiting. Each bead was coated with the same amount of hydrocarbons as one patroller ant.

Using tweezers, Greene and his colleagues took turns squatting at the nest entrance. Every ten seconds or so, one of them dropped one smelly bead into the nest. They dropped as many beads as the number of patrollers they had removed.[8] They just mimicked what would happen if patrollers walked back to the nest. Would the foragers leave the nest or stay inside?

> **Meet the Scientists:**
> *Deborah M. Gordon and Michael Greene are myrmecologists, or ant experts, at Stanford University, California. They study how different members of ant colonies communicate with one another to carry out the daily activities needed for the colony to survive and grow.*

Two harvester ants smell each other's heads with their antennae.

Smelling the Difference

The results were impressive. Foragers waiting in the nest entrance touched the beads with their antennae and then came out and foraged for the rest of the day. They behaved in the same way as when they touched patrollers coming back to the nest.

On the other hand, when foragers smelled the scent of maintenance workers on the beads (or no scent at all), they did not leave the nest. They responded in the same way as when patrollers did not come back to the nest. It was the patrollers' scent, and not the scent from other workers, that prompted foragers to begin their activities. This was not the whole story, though.

Detecting the scent alone was not enough to trigger foragers to leave and look for seeds. To trigger foraging, the scented beads also had to be dropped at a pace foragers seemed to recognize. Detecting just one bead coated with a patroller's scent did not trigger foraging. But detecting one bead every ten seconds seemed sufficient for foragers to go out of the nest and begin foraging.[9]

Gordon and her colleagues had uncovered one of the red harvester ants' secrets. Forager ants smell specific scents with their antennae on patrollers' bodies. When foragers smell the right message—a patroller scent repeatedly—then they leave the nest to gather food. But if the message is not quite right, like a different scent or only a single occurrence of the scent, then they stay home for the rest of the day.

3
ANTS GO TO SURVIVAL SCHOOL

Tom Richardson and Nigel Franks are coming back from the field with their hands full of ants. They are carefully bringing whole ant colonies to the lab where they will give them a home. The scientists hope that the ants will help them study a behavior that has intrigued researchers for many years: tandem running.

Here is an example of tandem running: A little worker ant finds a large source of food, like a pile of crumbs. The ant runs back to the nest and contacts another worker. Then the two ants head back to the food running in tandem, one right behind the other. The ant that found the crumbs leads the one that does not know where the food is.

Each ant carries a crumb back to the nest. Then each ant recruits another worker and leads it to the crumbs, running in tandem pairs as before. In time, many workers know where the crumbs are and carry them back home. You may think, what is so intriguing about that?

Touch and Go

This one-on-one recruitment sounds like a simple thing, but Richardson and Franks thought there was more to tandem running than meets the eye. When they observed ants closely in the wild, it did not look like the leader ant was just rushing back to the food and the other one was following right behind. The leader led the way, but it stopped when the follower got too far behind. When the follower got closer to the leader again, it tapped the leader's legs or abdomen with its antennae. Then the leader resumed running.[1] (The abdomen is the section of an ant's body farthest away from the head.)

> **Meet the Scientists:**
> *Nigel Franks and Tom Richardson are myrmecologists, or ant experts, at Bristol University in England. They are interested in understanding the different ways ants communicate with one another.*

If the follower got far behind again, the leader stopped and waited for the follower to tap it before restarting running. By tapping the leader with its antennae, the follower appeared to signal that it was back on track, and both continued on their way.

The touch-and-go strategy suggested to Richardson and Franks that the leader ant was doing more than returning to the food. Instead, it seemed that the leader was teaching the follower the route that led to the food. The leader waited for the follower when it lagged behind, making sure it would learn the way to the food. But was it really teaching?

Professor Ant?

Some animals can learn new skills by simply observing another perform that skill. For example, chimpanzees insert thin tree branches into termite nests to "fish," eating the delicious insects that crawl onto the branch.[2] In this case, an adult chimp does not seem to spend time teaching a young chimp the skill. Young chimpanzees simply observe and imitate the adults' behavior.

People, too, can learn by imitating others. We also learn when a person spends time teaching us something new. Teaching this way requires two-way communication between teacher and student. The teacher demonstrates the skill and watches the student perform it. The student communicates with the teacher, so he or she continues teaching. Richardson and Franks wondered if tandem running could be the ants' way of teaching.

The scientists reasoned that for an animal to teach another, there had to be two-way communication between them. This would allow the teacher to recognize if the student was learning or not. The scientists thought that tandem running was an ant's way of teaching another where food was. They just had to prove that the touch-and-go strategy was a two-way communication.

Fast Ants

To show that the leader and the follower ant had a two-way communication, the scientists measured the distance between the ants as they ran in tandem toward the food. Then they compared this with their speed.[3]

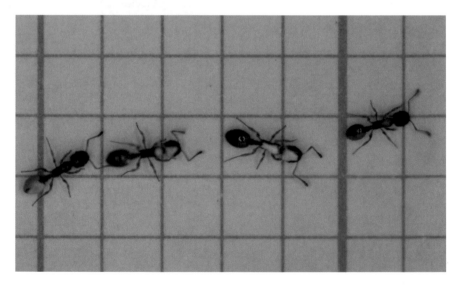

Pairs of ants tandem running over 2 millimeter (0.08 inch) squares so the scientists can calculate the ants' speed and distance from each other. When the distance between two ants is larger than the length of their antenna, the pair adjusts their speed to remain in touch.

If there was two-way communication, the scientists expected that the leader and the follower would respond to antennal contact in a way that allowed them to stay together. If the distance between the ants increased so much that the follower could not touch the leader with its antennae, then the scientists expected the leader to slow down or stop. They also expected the follower to speed up in order to catch up. If the ants were close enough for the follower to touch the leader, then the scientists expected that both ants would keep running at the same speed.[4]

Ants are very quick, both with their legs and their antennae. Measuring ants' speed and the distance between them as they run is not an easy thing to do in the wild. That is why Richardson and Franks decided to bring the ants to their lab. They did the experiments in a foraging arena.

The foraging arena consisted of a round surface with a grid printed on it. This helped the scientists measure the ants' speed and the distance between them. The scientists also used cameras to videotape the ants. The cameras allowed the scientists to study the action very slowly—frame by frame— and very closely.[5]

From Head to Abdomen

Using the camera, the scientists determined the distance between the ants during tandem running. They measured the distance between the follower's head and the leader's abdomen.

The scientists first thought about measuring the distance between the follower's antennae and the leader's abdomen. But the antennae were too fast to be clearly visible in the video recording. Instead, they measured the distance between the head and the abdomen, which was possible to do.

They also measured the length of the antennae of each follower they studied (the ant was cooled down so it stayed still, but not harmed, while they measured the antennae). This determined whether the follower was within contact range. Now the scientists were ready to do their experiment.

Before beginning tandem running, one ant shares a drop of liquid (perhaps water) with another ant. Then the leader begins tandem running to show the follower where to find more.

School Is On!

Franks and Richardson placed two ants on the foraging arena. One of the ants, the leader, already knew where to find food (sugared water). The second ant did not know where the food was.

The ants ran in tandem, the cameras rolled, and the scientists observed the fast ants perform this intriguing behavior. They saw many pairs of ants running in tandem and videotaped them all. After analyzing the videos frame by frame and calculating the ants' speeds and the distances between them, the scientists were very pleased.

The data backed up their hypothesis. When the distance between the follower's head and the leader's abdomen was too long for the antennae to touch it, the leader slowed down and the follower sped up. When the distance between both ants allowed for antennal contact, both ants ran at about the same speed.[6]

Franks and Richardson had uncovered a well-hidden ant secret. They think that these ants use tandem running to teach each other where to find food. Using the antennae to stay in contact, leader and forager adjust their speed as they run. This allows the follower to learn the way to the food and teach it to others. Ants have a small brain, but it certainly is enough to get a one-on-one education!

UP, DOWN, AND BACKWARD

Temnothorax albipennis sometimes uses tandem running to teach other ants where food or home is; however, these ants may also just carry a nest mate upside down and looking backward, and take it to a food source or shelter. When this happens, the carried ants do not teach others later on. The scientists think that is because they cannot learn the way being upside down and looking backward. On the other hand, another species of ants carries nest mates with their heads upright. In this case, the carried ants seem to learn the route and later teach others.

How Fast Is It Going?

Many scientists have to measure how fast animals travel. Today, they have various instruments available that allow them to measure speed accurately. But how would you do it if you did not have access to those tools? In this activity you will measure how fast a small object travels using a simple method.

Materials
★ large poster board
★ ruler
★ markers
★ small racing car or small ball
★ chronometer or a watch that measures seconds
★ a partner to assist with the experiment

Procedure

1. Draw a grid on the poster board using the ruler and markers. Make each square on the grid 10 x 10 centimeters (about 4 x 4 inches). Mark one end of the poster board "Beginning" and the opposite side "End."

2. Place the grid flat on the floor.

3. Have your partner roll the ball or slide the racing car over the grid as straight as possible, trying to reach the "End" zone.

4. When your partner says "Go!" and the object begins to travel over the grid, begin timing with the chronometer or watch. Stop timing when the object stops or passes the "End."

5. Repeat the test, this time pushing the car or the ball with more or less force to increase or reduce its speed on the grid; find the object's speed after slightly inclining the grid.

6. Count the number of squares the object passed as it traveled over the grid. Record the time each run took. Record the results in the following table (you may add more tests by inclining the board at different angles):

Test #	Number of squares traveled	Time (seconds)	Speed = number of squares divided by time (squares/seconds or centimeters [inches]/seconds)
1. Flat			
2. Flat, pushing with more or less force			
3. Inclined grid			

Calculating the speed of the object:

Speed is the distance traveled by an object per unit of time.

$$\text{Speed} = \frac{\text{distance}}{\text{time}}$$

For example, if you jog 1 kilometer (about 0.6 miles) in 4 minutes, your speed will be:

$$\text{Speed} = \frac{1 \text{ kilometer}}{4 \text{ minutes}} = 0.25 \text{ kilometer (0.2 miles)/minute}$$

Use the same formula above to calculate the different speeds of the objects tested on the board. For example, if the ball rolled over 10 squares on the board in 5 seconds, then its speed will be:

$$\text{Speed} = \frac{10 \text{ squares}}{5 \text{ seconds}} = 2 \text{ squares/second}$$

You may be more precise in your calculations by replacing the number of squares with distance. One square is 10 centimeters (4 inches), so 10 squares will be 100 centimeters (40 inches).

$$\text{Speed} = \frac{100 \text{ centimeters}}{5 \text{ seconds}} = 20 \text{ centimeters (8 inches)/second}$$

4
IN DEVIL'S GARDENS, ANTS RULE

The locals did not want anything to do with them, but Megan Frederickson was very intrigued by devil's gardens. For the people living in Madre Selva (Mother Forest) in the Amazon rain forest in western Perú, it appeared that someone had made the gardens. It looked like someone had cleared out patches of all the ground vegetation on the thick forest floor. Then someone had planted a single type of spindly tree called *Duroia hirsuta*. Some gardens have hundreds of this kind of tree.

The locals knew that they certainly had not cleared out such areas in the rain forest. They concluded that an evil spirit called Chuyachaqui in the native Quechua language must tend the devil's gardens. Megan Frederickson and

Deborah Gordon had a different idea about how devil's gardens came to be. They thought that the local ants had something to do with it.[1]

Of Ants and Trees

Duroia trees that populate devil's gardens have an interesting companion called *Myrmelachista* ants. The ants nest inside hollow, swollen structures in the stems or leaf pouches of the *Duroia*. Millions of ants, each 3 millimeters (1/8 inch) long, live inside the trees, caring for thousands of queens.

The trees and the ants depend on each other completely. Scientists call them obligate partners because they would perish

Close view of *Myrmelachista* ants attacking saplings of a different tree than the *Duroia* that were recently planted in the devil's garden. The ants have climbed unprotected saplings, biting their young stems and injecting deadly formic acid.

without each other. Ants and trees live together in the gardens for many years. Frederickson has estimated that some gardens might be eight hundred years old![2] How do they prevent the numerous plants in the surrounding rain forest from growing in the garden?

Scientists had two hypotheses, or ideas, to explain the existence of devil's gardens. One idea was that *Duroia* trees release a toxic chemical into the soil that kills plants that attempt to invade

the garden. Scientists call this plant-kill-plant strategy allelopathy. The second idea was that the ants, not the trees, kill other plants that try to settle in the garden. Frederickson tested the last hypothesis.

Saplings in Danger

For several years, Frederickson worked on as many as ten different devil's gardens in the Peruvian Amazon forest. She tried to determine if the ants were involved in the creation and maintenance of the gardens.

One of her experiments consisted of planting saplings, or young plants, of a different kind inside the garden to see what would happen to them. Frederickson planted saplings of a common Amazonian tree called Spanish cedar near the base of a *Duroia* tree actively patrolled by worker ants.

An area of a devil's garden showing only one type of thin tree (*Duroia*) and the ground practically clear of vegetation. Compare the garden with the thick rain forest vegetation in the background.

Frederickson protected some of the saplings from the ants with a caramel-colored product that is very sticky called Tanglefoot. This sticky, waterproof barrier prevented the ants from getting on the saplings. She left other cedar saplings unprotected; the ants had easy access to them.[3]

Formidable Formica

Frederickson did not have to wait long for the results. Worker ants quickly attacked the unprotected saplings. They climbed toward the leaves and applied formic acid. This is a chemical these ants produce and store inside their bodies. An ant would chew a hole into a leaf stem and then drop the acid inside the hole from the tip of its abdomen.[4]

Formic acid turned out to be very poisonous to the invading trees. The poisoned saplings lost most of their leaves within five days and died. On the other hand, the saplings of Spanish cedar that were protected with Tanglefoot survived. The barrier prevented the ants from reaching the leaves and applying the poison.[5]

To confirm that formic acid was the poison responsible for the saplings' deaths, the scientists applied formic acid directly to healthy leaves. The leaves began dying, just like the ones that the ants had poisoned. The scientists also confirmed that the only chemical the ants had applied was formic acid, nothing else. Formic acid derives its name from the Latin word *formica*, which means "ant."[6]

The consistent results showed Frederickson that the ants killed the saplings of all plants except the *Duroia*. It was not *Duroia* that poisoned the soil; the ants were the keepers of the devil's gardens. This was the first time that it had been reported that ants used formic acid as a herbicide, or plant killer.

Helping Each Other

Frederickson and Gordon had discovered the secret of devil's gardens. *Myrmelachista* ant colonies build a home for themselves by creating devil's gardens slowly over years. The ants

Megan Frederickson in the Peruvian Amazon heading toward devil's gardens to continue her research.

find a single *Duroia* tree and make a nest in it. Then the ants begin killing plants of other species growing around the *Duroia*. As plants die, they leave open spaces and plenty of sunshine for new *Duroia* plants to grow. More *Duroia* plants create new nest homes for the ants. The process continues over the years.[7]

    Duroia plants and *Myrmelachista* ants seem to have a perfect deal that benefits both of them. Scientists call this type of arrangement a mutualistic relationship. The plants provide a nesting place and food for the ants, while the ants clear the land of other plants that may compete with the *Duroia* for space and sunlight.

5
AN ARMY OF ONE

Scott Powell and Nigel Franks could not see them yet, but they heard them coming. Breaking the early morning silence at Barro Colorado Island in Panamá, a swarm of two hundred thousand reddish black army ants steadily advances over ground littered with twigs, leaves, and other natural obstacles.

There is rattling and ruffling of leaves and vegetation as the ants scurry along and agitated creatures get flushed out. There is the tap-tap of insects randomly jumping on leaves and wood as they try to escape from the swarm.

> **Meet the Scientists:**
> **Nigel Franks and Scott Powell are myrmecologists, or ant experts, at Bristol University in England. They study how ants help each other for the good of the colony.**

35

There is the fluttering of birds trying to catch some of the prey. The noises increase, mix, and continue for hours as the swarm moves on. Sometimes rain soaks the ground and muffles the sounds.

A Swarm of Predators

The army ants swarm is shaped like a fan. It can be as wide as one and a half adult soccer goals (about 10 meters or 33 feet) and as long as the average height of professional basketball players (2 meters or about 6.6 feet)! The narrow end of the huge, fan-shaped swarm continues like a tail, making a trail of about 91 meters (100 yards), as long as a football field. It leads back to the nest.

This trail is a two-way, three-lane highway through which these virtually blind ants go back and forth carrying prey. The ants leaving the nest use the two outer lanes, while the returning ants use the center lane. They find their way by following a trail of chemicals called pheromones.[1] At the end of the day, these carnivorous ants retreat to their nest. The next day, they break the morning silence again as the swarm moves forward raiding along a new path on the ground. The raids capture thousands of varied prey, including tarantulas, scorpions, beetles, roaches, and grasshoppers.[2] They have to if

Science Tongue Twister:
Franks and Powell studied an army ant species called **Eciton burchellii.**

A bivouac (or temporary nest) of a huge colony of the army ant *Eciton burchellii*.

the whole colony of seven hundred thousand ants is going to survive.

There Are Potholes Everywhere

Powell and Franks have been fascinated by the way army ants carry on their raids and travel faster than other ants along trails. To study the ants at Barro Colorado Island, they used a video camera to film the ants speeding along the two-way, three-lane tracks.

When they watched the videos, the scientists' witnessed an intriguing scene. The trails the ants followed were covered with leaves, twigs, and other obstacles that created an irregular surface. There were many potholes along the way, which slowed down the ants' traffic.

What caught the scientists' interest was that many of the potholes were plugged by live ants. The ants spread their bodies over the potholes, holding on to the edges with their long, claw-tipped legs. This created a living plug over which the other ants hurried carrying their prey.[3] What a curious observation!

Were the ants using their bodies to plug the holes and therefore create a smoother surface to run over? Or had the poor ants just fallen into the pothole?

The Experimental Apparatus

Powell and Franks decided to study the pothole-plugging behavior in the wild. It would be extremely difficult to recreate the swarming behavior of several hundred thousand ants in the lab. Studying this behavior in the wild, however, was also challenging.

Natural trails are very variable. The scientists could not have reached any conclusions if they had to compare trails that varied in many ways, like in the number and size of potholes. They solved this problem by creating their own artificial trails and having the ants travel over them.

They built an experimental apparatus. It looked like two ramps, one in front of the other, connected by a rectangular plank. They built different types of planks, and they could

Ants plugging holes with their bodies over the experimental apparatus. Dr. Powell took this photo with a slow shutter and natural light, giving crisp focus to the plug ants while the fast-moving foragers are blurred.

interchange them. One plank was smooth and had no potholes in it. The second plank had small potholes, 6 millimeters (0.24 inch) in diameter, and the third plank had larger potholes, 10 millimeters (0.4 inch) in diameter.[4]

The scientists placed the experimental apparatus on the ant trail, and the ant traffic redirected over it. As the ants sped up over the plank the scientists filmed their behavior.

Fitting the Plugs

The scientists measured the speed of the ants traveling over the plank without potholes. They compared it with the speed

Ants plugging holes with their bodies over the experimental apparatus. Dr. Powell took this photo with slow shutter speed and a quick flash at the beginning, to register the fast moving foragers as ghostly outlines.

of the ants rushing over the planks with small and large potholes. The videos showed what the ants did when they encountered potholes on their way.

When an ant that was not carrying prey encountered a pothole, it first used its antennae to detect the size of the pothole. The ant crawled around the edges of the pothole, touching it with its antennae. If the ants behind the "plugging ant" walked over it, the plugging ant spread its legs while rocking back and forth.

If the ant covered the pothole well, then it would stop moving (except for the antennae). If the ant was too big to fit into the pothole, it continued on its way. If the ant was too small to cover the pothole completely, it remained and covered part of the pothole. Then another ant filled the remaining space. One ant was enough to plug the small potholes in the plank. Two or three ants plugged the larger potholes.[5]

***Eciton burchellii* workers forming "ant-plugs" in gaps in the leaf-litter, allowing foragers to run over them.**

Smooth Roads Mean Speedy Delivery

It is true. Army ants use their bodies to plug potholes on their trails. But, if ants are plugging potholes, then they are not available to carry food. Is this really useful to the colony?

The scientists measured the ants' speed over a smooth (no potholes) plank and compared it to their speed on planks with potholes. They found that the ants were faster on the smooth plank. Traveling over potholes slowed down the ants. However, after ants plugged the potholes with their bodies, the ants rushing over them ran almost as fast as the ants running over the smooth plank.[6] In the long run, the pothole-plugging behavior helps deliver more food to the nest, which benefits the whole colony.

The scientists uncovered the army ants' secret. Ants in this huge colony help all their nest mates by becoming living pothole plugs. Covering the potholes on the trail creates smoother tracks on which ants can speed up and deliver precious food for the whole colony.

★ CHAPTER NOTES ★

Chapter 1. Bugs Squeeze to Breathe

1. Greg Borzo, "Field Museum, Argonne Lab Harness Powerful X-rays in New Technique to Study Animal Functions. Researchers Discover Insect Breathing Mechanism," *The Field Museum Press Release*, January 2003, <http://www.fieldmuseum.org/museum_info/press/press_insect.htm> (December 17, 2007).
2. Ibid.
3. Personal interview with Dr. Wah-Keat Lee, July 2, 2007.
4. John J. Socha et al., "Real-time Phase-contrast X-ray Imaging: A New Technique for the Study of Animal Form and Function," *BioMed Central*, vol. 5, no. 6, March 1, 2007, <http://www.pubmedcentral.nih.gov/picrender.fcgi?artid=1831761&blob-type=pdf> (December 17, 2007).
5. John R. Meyer, "Insect Physiology. Respiratory System," online tutorial, North Carolina State University, November 1, 2006, <http://www.cals.ncsu.edu/course/ent425/tutorial/respire.html> (December 17, 2007).
6. Mark W. Westneat et al., "Tracheal Respiration in Insects Visualized With Synchrotron X-ray Imaging," *Science*, vol. 299, no. 5606, January 24, 2003, p. 558.
7. Ibid., p. 559.
8. Borzo.

Chapter 2. Ants Have Business Cards

1. Deborah Gordon, *Ants at Work: How an Insect Society Is Organized* (New York: The Free Press, 1999), p. 3.
2. Ibid., p. 28.
3. Ibid., pp. 32–33.
4. Personal interview with Dr. Deborah Gordon, June 28, 2007.

5. Gordon, p. 13.

6. Michael Greene and Deborah M. Gordon, "Cuticular Hydrocarbons Inform Task Decisions," *Nature*, vol. 423, no. 6935, May 1, 2003, p. 32.

7. Ibid.

8. Ibid.

9. Ibid.

Chapter 3. Ants Go to Survival School

1. Nigel R. Franks and Tom Richardson, "Teaching in Tandem-running Ants. Tapping Into the Dialogue Between Leader and Follower Reveals an Unexpected Social Skill," *Nature*, vol. 439, January 12, 2006, p. 153.

2. Crickette Sanz, Dave Morgan, and Steve Gulick, "New Insights Into Chimpanzees, Tools, and Termites From the Congo Basin," *The American Naturalist*, vol. 164, no. 5, November 2004, pp. 567–581, (see illustrations and photos, pp. 572–575), <http://www.journals.uchicago.edu/doi/abs/10.1086/424803> (December 17, 2007).

3. Franks and Richardson, p. 153.

4. Personal interview with Dr. Tom Richardson, July 2, 2007.

5. Franks and Richardson, p. 153.

6. Ibid.

Chapter 4. In Devil's Gardens, Ants Rule

1. Megan E. Frederickson, Michael J. Greene, and Deborah M. Gordon, "Devil's Gardens' Bedevilled by Ants," *Nature*, vol. 437, September 22, 2005, p. 495.

2. Ibid.

3. Ibid.

4. Personal interview with Dr. Deborah Gordon, June 28, 2007.

5. Frederickson, Greene, and Gordon, p. 495.

6. "Raising the Devil: Amazon Ants Poison Unwanted Plants," *The Journal of Young Investigators*, vol. 18, no. 1, September 22,

2005, <http://www.jyi.org/news/nb.php?id=557> (December 17, 2007).

7. Frederickson, Greene, and Gordon, p. 496.

Chapter 5. An Army of One

1. Iain D. Couzin and Nigel R. Franks, "Self-Organized Lane Formation and Optimized Traffic Flow in Army Ants," *Proceedings of the Royal Society London B*, vol. 270, no. 1511, January 22, 2003, pp. 139–146, <http://journals.royalsociety.org/content/w1v5wt0e6cvncnp3/fulltext.pdf> (December 17, 2007).

2. Personal interview with Dr. Scott Powell, July 8, 2007.

3. Scott Powell and Nigel R. Franks, "How a Few Help All: Living Pothole Plugs Speed Prey Delivery in the Army Ant *Eciton burchellii*," *Animal Behavior*, vol. 73, no. 6, June 2007, p. 1068.

4. Ibid., p. 1069.

5. Ibid., p. 1071, Figure 2.

6. Ibid., p. 1072.

★ GLOSSARY ★

abdomen ★ The section of the ant's body opposite to the head.

allelopathy ★ The inhibition of growth of one species of plants by chemicals produced by another species of plants.

Chuyachaqui (choo-ya-CHA-kee) ★ An evil spirit in the Quechua language of Peruvian Indians believed to be the keeper of the devil's gardens.

cuticle ★ The hardened covering on the outside of the body of many invertebrates, like insects.

formica ★ The Latin name for ant.

formic acid ★ A chemical produced by some ants.

hydrocarbons ★ Organic compounds that only contain carbon and hydrogen.

mutualistic ★ A word that describes the relationship between two organisms that benefits both.

myrmecologist ★ A scientist that studies ants.

pheromones ★ Chemicals produced by one animal that affects the behavior of others.

spiracles ★ Openings on the body surface of insects through which air enters and exits.

synchrotron ★ A powerful machine that produces very intense X-rays.

tracheae ★ Tubes that form the airways of air-breathing animals.

★ FURTHER READING ★

Books

Markle, Sandra. *Army Ants*. Minneapolis, Minn.: Lerner Publishers, 2005.

Taylor, Barbara. *Insects*. Boston: Kingfisher, 2006.

Whiting, Sue. *All About Ants*. Washington, D.C.: National Geographic, 2006.

Zabludoff, Marc. *The Insect Class*. New York: Marshall Cavendish Benchmark, 2006.

Internet Addresses

Live Science: All About Insects
http://www.livescience.com/insects/

The Wonderful World of Insects
http://www.earthlife.net/insects/

Video of tracheae moving in live insects
http://www.aps.anl.gov/News/APS_News/2003/Images/20030127a.avi

Ana María Rodríguez's Homepage
http://www.anamariarodriguez.com/

★ INDEX ★